W9-BKL-862

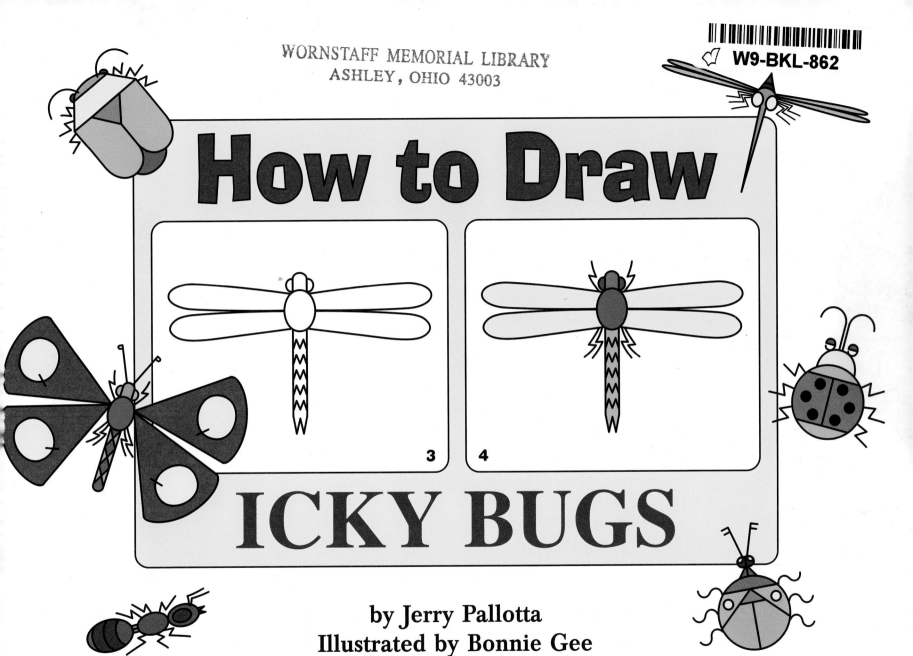

How to Draw

3 4

ICKY BUGS

by Jerry Pallotta
Illustrated by Bonnie Gee

SCHOLASTIC INC.

New York   Toronto   London   Auckland   Sydney   Mexico City   New Delhi   Hong Kong   Buenos Aires

Extra special thanks to Malph Rasiello.

—— Jerry Pallotta

To my budding little artist, Michael; my husband; family; and friends.

——Bonnie Gee

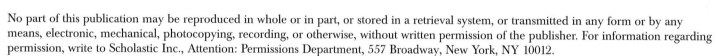

ISBN 0-439-38916-X

12 11 10 9 8 7 6 5 4 3 2   3 4 5 6 7 8/0

Printed in the U.S.A.   08

First printing, October 2003

If you want to learn how to draw Icky Bugs, all you need is the alphabet. You will also need some paper and a pen, pencil, crayon, or marker. Are you ready to draw some Icky Bugs? When you finish drawing them, feel free to color them in.

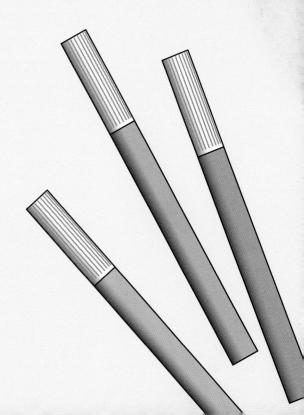

ABCDEFG
HIJKLMNOP
QRSTUV
WXYZ

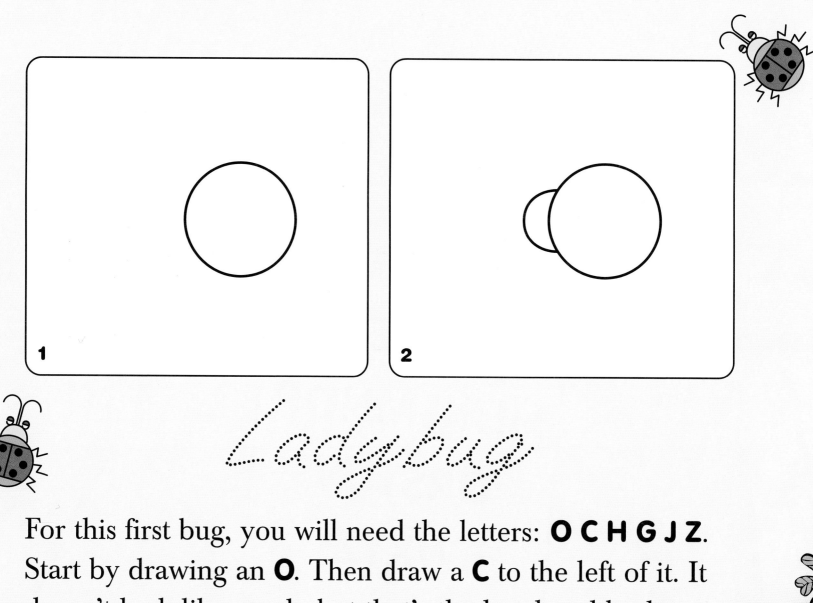

Ladybug

For this first bug, you will need the letters: **O C H G J Z**. Start by drawing an **O**. Then draw a **C** to the left of it. It doesn't look like much, but that's the head and body.

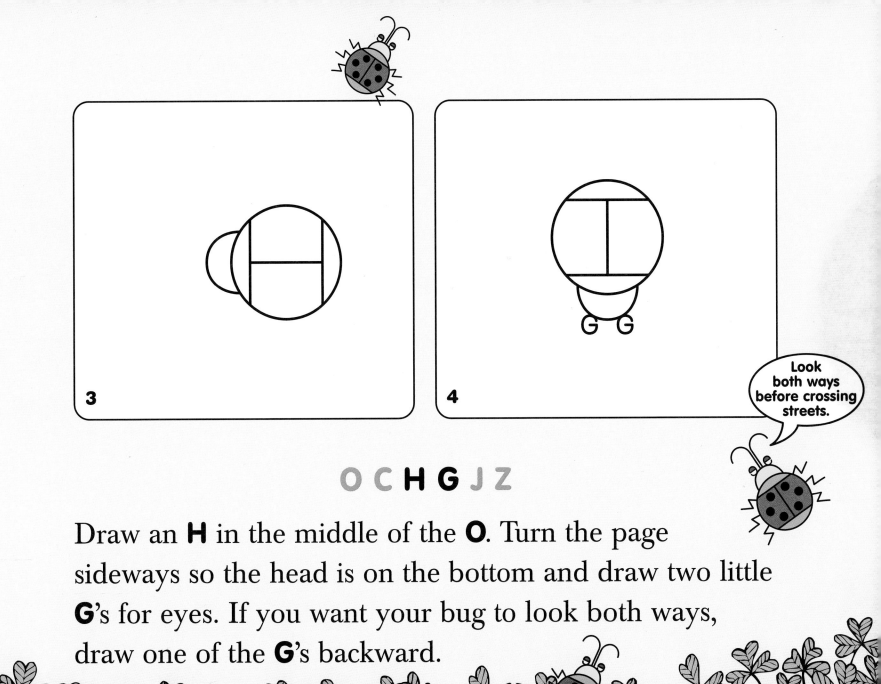

O C **H** **G** J Z

Draw an **H** in the middle of the **O**. Turn the page sideways so the head is on the bottom and draw two little **G**'s for eyes. If you want your bug to look both ways, draw one of the **G**'s backward.

Look both ways before crossing streets.

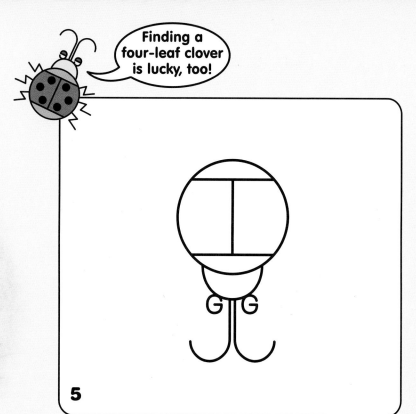

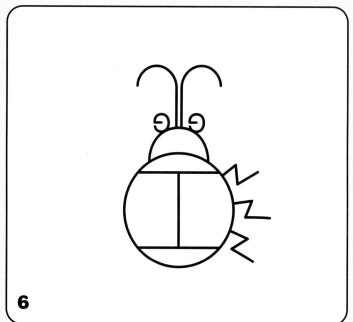

O C H G **J Z**

Draw a **J** in between the eyes and a backward **J** next to it. Now turn the paper so the head is on top. Let's make this bug an insect. All insects have six legs. So, first, draw three **Z**'s on the right side of the body.

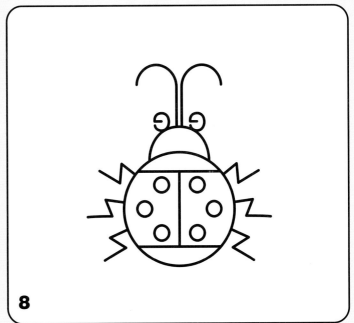

O C H G J **Z**

Here is the tricky part of our first bug. Draw three backward **Z**'s on the left side. If you want to get fancy, you can draw more **O**'s on your bug. This ladybug is our first Icky Bug. Icky bugs are awesome.

Mosquito

For this itchy bug, you will need the letters: **O U V A Z**.
First, draw two **O**'s close together. Those will be eyes.
Connect them on top with an upside-down **U**.

I love to bite!

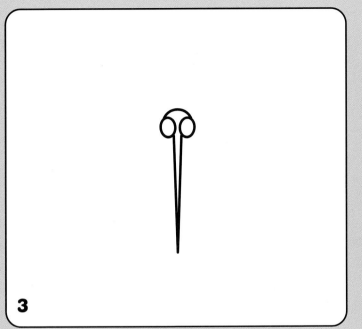

3

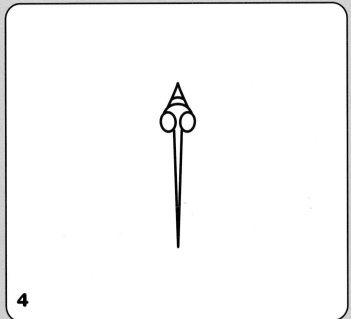

4

O U **V A** Z

Now draw a very skinny **V** in between the eyes.
Draw an **A** on top of the head. It's hard to see it now,
but that's its body.

I'm just
itching to
bite you!

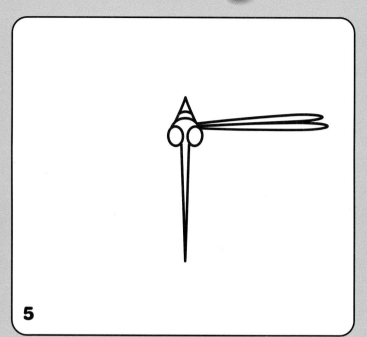

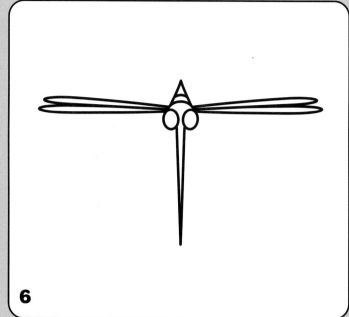

O U V A Z

To make wings, draw two very skinny **U**'s on the right side of the body. Draw two more on the left side. It's starting to buzz.

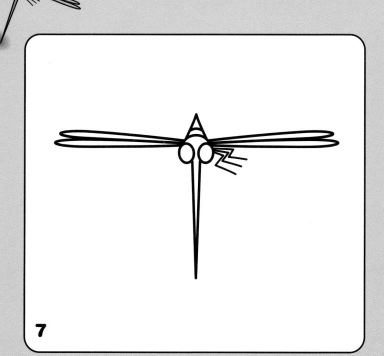

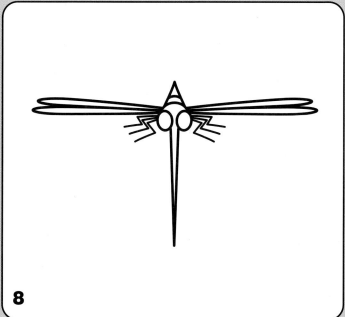

7

8

O U V A **Z**

For the legs, draw three **Z**'s on the right side, under the wing. Then draw three backward **Z**'s on the left side. Hurry up and turn the page before it bites you!

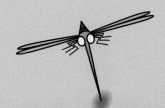

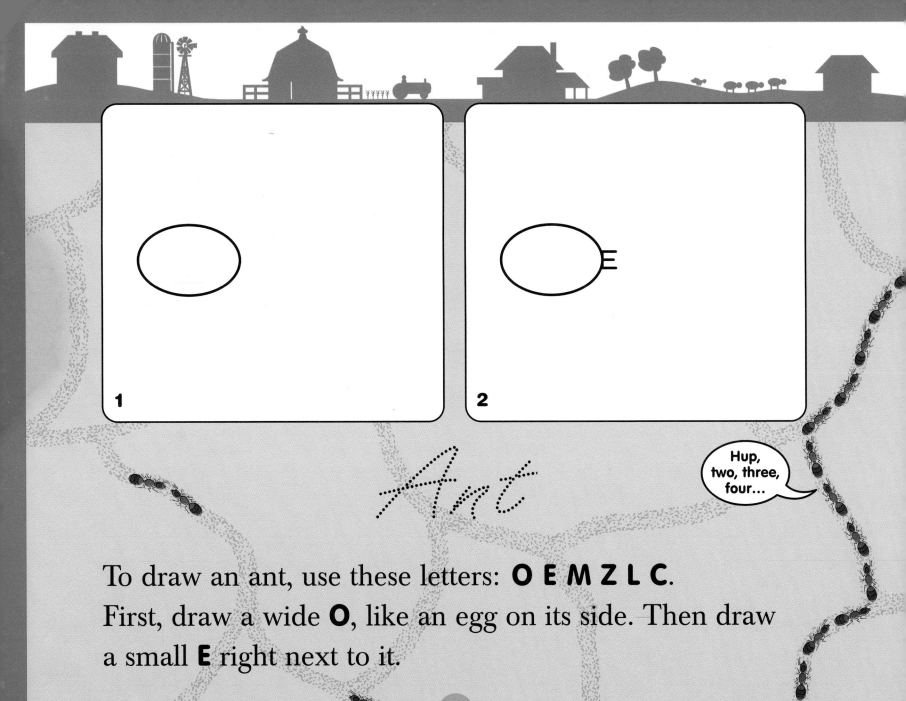

To draw an ant, use these letters: **O E M Z L C**.

First, draw a wide **O**, like an egg on its side. Then draw a small **E** right next to it.

O E M Z L C

Make two smaller **O**'s on the right, just touching each other. Then add a tiny, sideways **M** for a mouth.

O E M **Z** L C

Make the bottom legs with **Z**'s or backward **Z**'s. Do the same for the top legs. Insects have three main body parts: head, thorax, abdomen. The legs should be drawn coming out of the thorax.

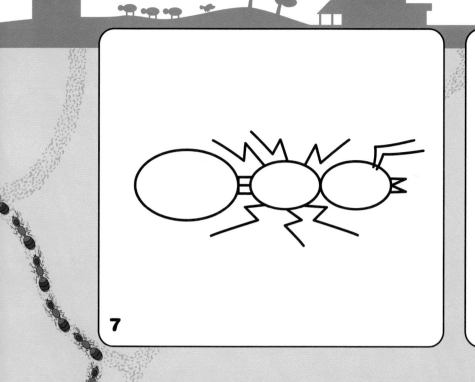

O E M Z L C

Draw two sideways **L**'s on the top of the head for antennae. Draw some **C**'s on the abdomen and an **O** on the head to complete your ant.

I'm your aunt!

No! You're an ANT.

True Bug

You can tell a true bug by the **Y** in the middle of its back. You will need the letters: **B Y I C Z**. Draw the letter **B**. Then turn it to the right, facing down, and draw a **Y** in the middle.

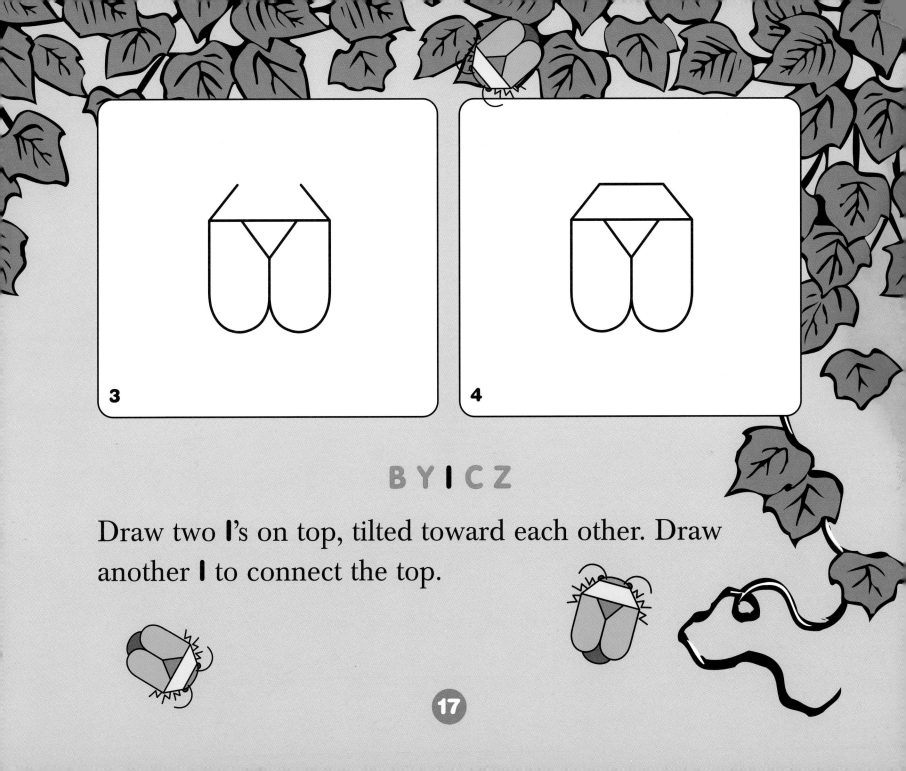

BY|CZ

Draw two **I**'s on top, tilted toward each other. Draw another **I** to connect the top.

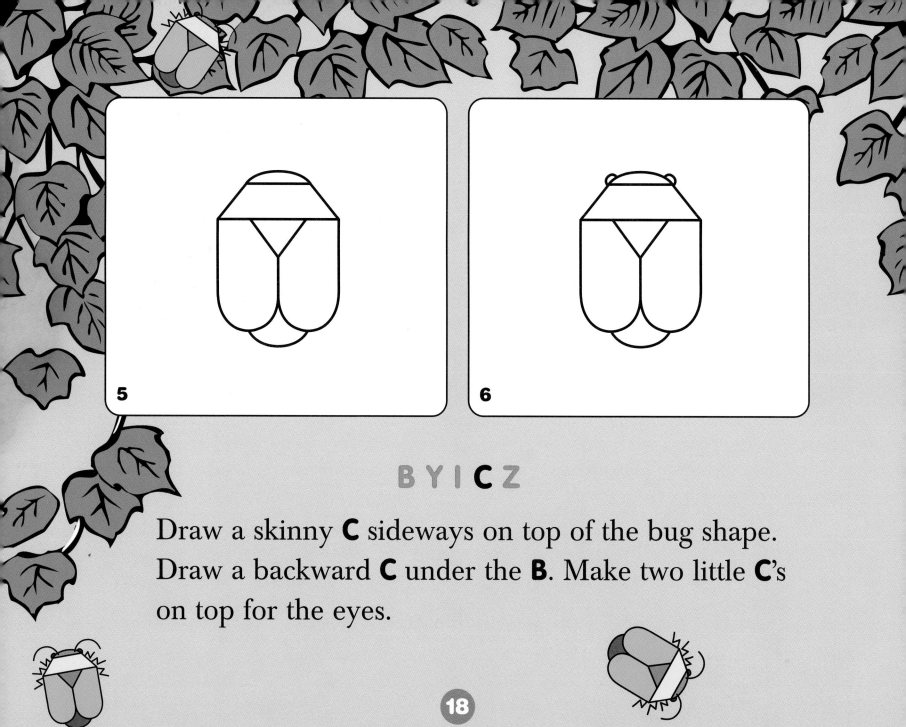

BYICZ

Draw a skinny **C** sideways on top of the bug shape. Draw a backward **C** under the **B**. Make two little **C**'s on top for the eyes.

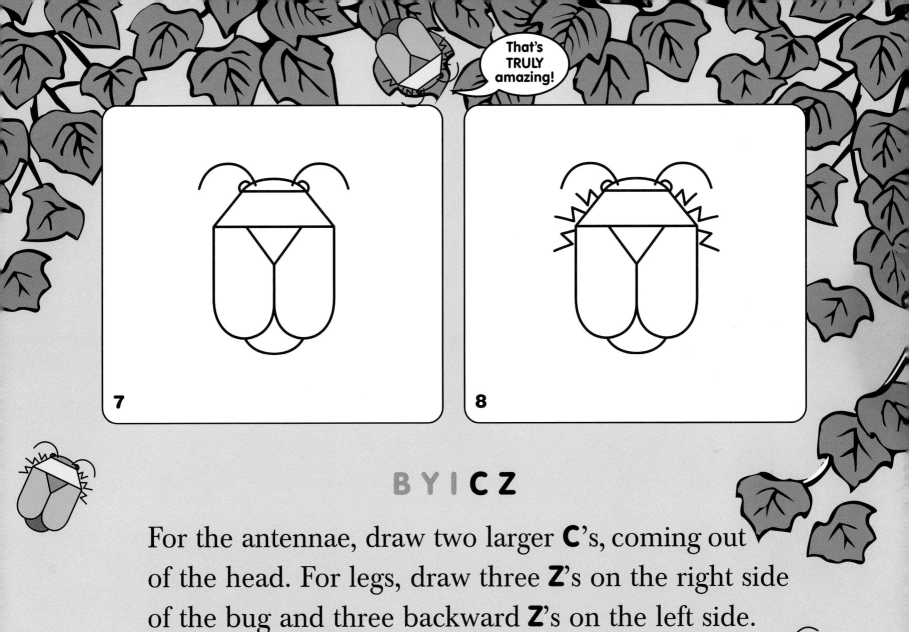

That's TRULY amazing!

B Y I C Z

For the antennae, draw two larger **C**'s, coming out of the head. For legs, draw three **Z**'s on the right side of the bug and three backward **Z**'s on the left side. There, you did it!

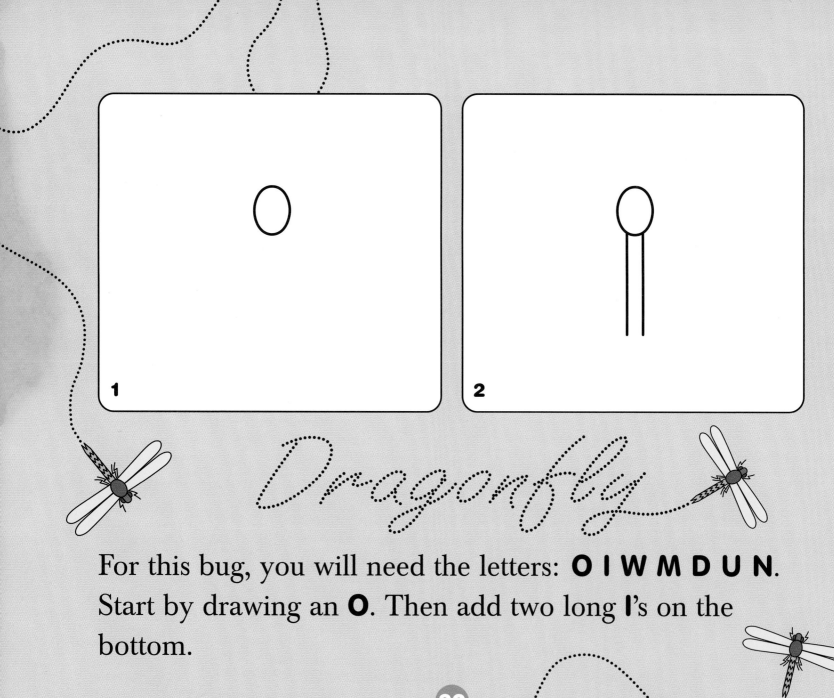

For this bug, you will need the letters: **O I W M D U N**.
Start by drawing an **O**. Then add two long **I**'s on the
bottom.

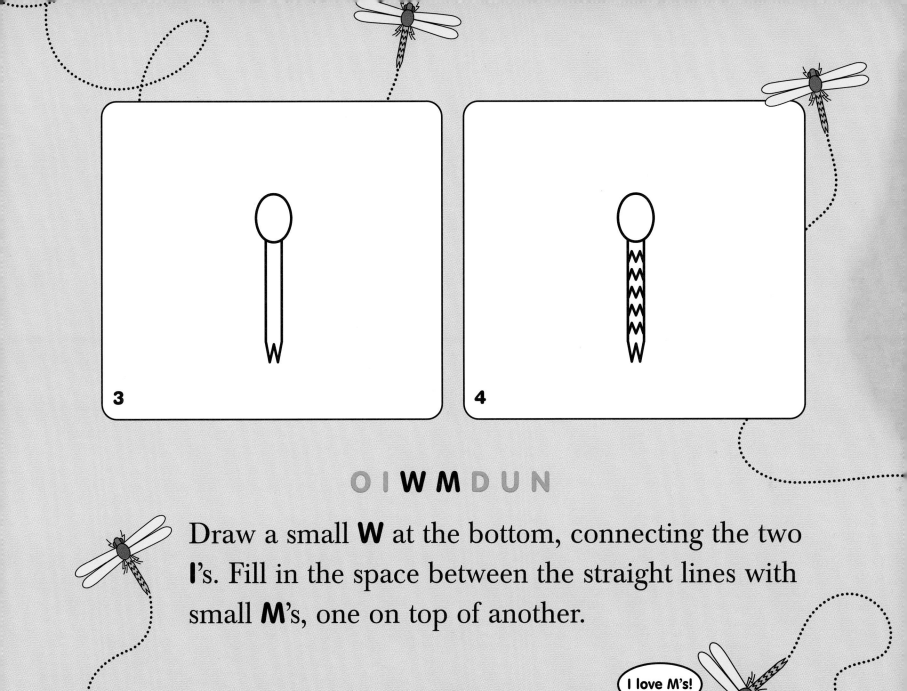

O I W M D U N

Draw a small **W** at the bottom, connecting the two
I's. Fill in the space between the straight lines with
small **M**'s, one on top of another.

I love M's!

21

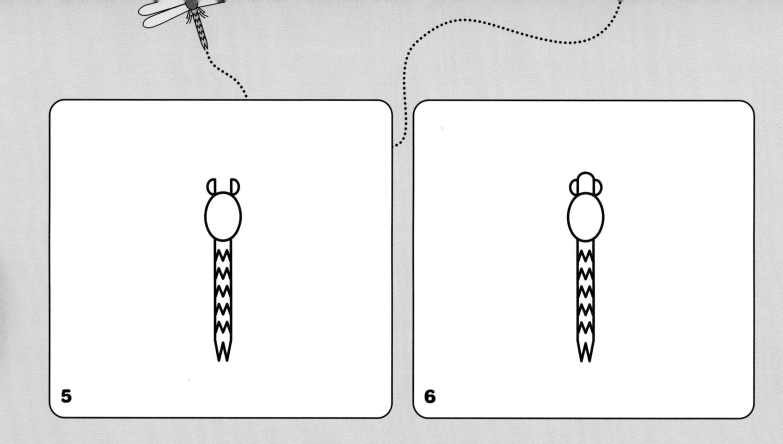

O I W M D U N

Draw a **D** and a backward **D**, lining up the straight parts of the **D** with the **I**'s below. Then add an upside-down **U** in between the two **D**'s.

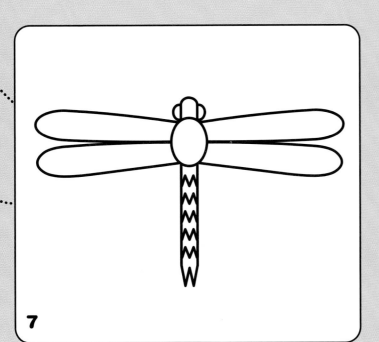

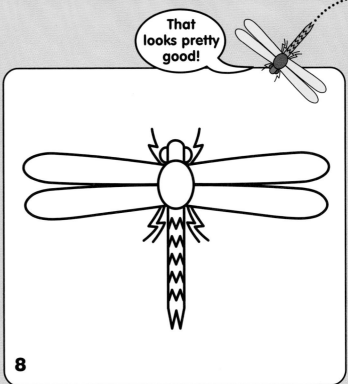

O I W M D U N

Draw two very long **U**'s sideways on each side of the **O** to make the wings. Make legs by drawing an **N** and a backward **N** on top of the wings by the head. Do the same at the bottom of the wings, but draw two on each side. The dragonfly is done!

1

2

Butterfly

To make a butterfly, you will need: **O D U X V Q P N**.
Whew! Better get started. First, draw an **O**, then two **D**'s
and an upside-down **U**, just like you did for the dragonfly.

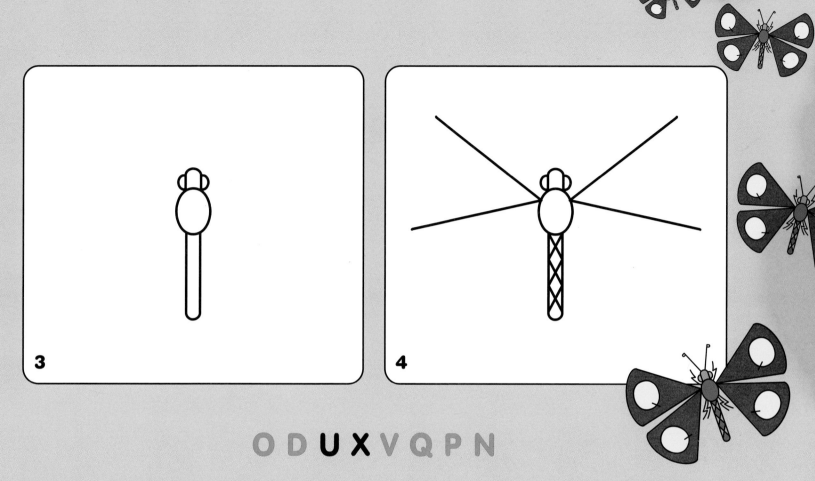

O D U X V Q P N

Draw a very long **U** underneath the body, and fill it in with **X**'s, one on top of another. For wings, draw **V**'s coming out of both sides of the body.

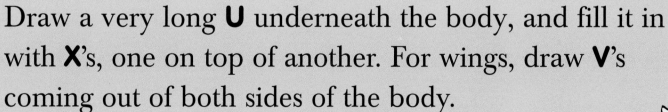

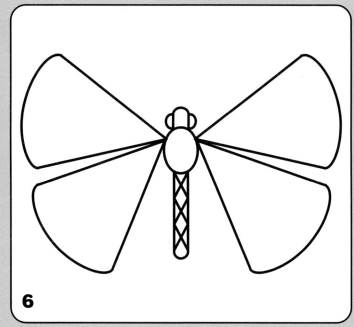

O D **U** X **X** **V** **Q** P N

Connect the top of each **V** with a flat, upside-down **U**. Now draw two more **V**'s underneath those wings, pointing slightly down. Draw two more **U**'s to connect those **V**'s and finish the wings.

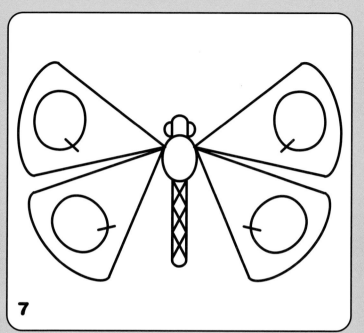

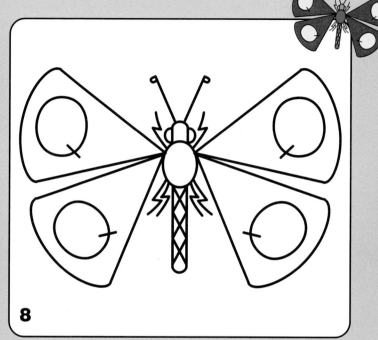

O D U X V **Q P N**

For a pattern, draw a **Q** on each of the left wings, and a backward **Q** on the right. Next, draw a tiny but long **P** on the right side of the head, and a backward **P** on the left. Finish it off with two **N**'s and two backward **N**'s for legs.

1

2

Alpha Beetle

To draw this bug, you will need the letters: **O K R T F S**. Start by drawing an **O**. Next, draw a **K** in the middle of the **O**, then turn the page sideways.

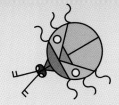

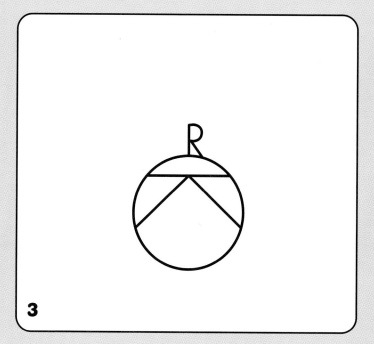

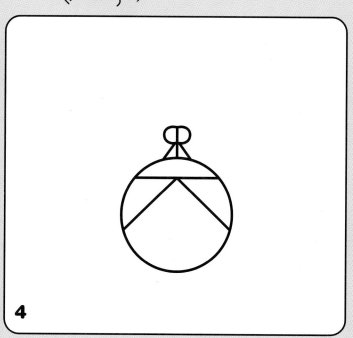

3

4

O K **R** T F S

Make a small **R** at the top of the bug, and a backward **R** right next to it. It doesn't look much like a bug, does it? Well, just wait till the end.

How s-wheat it is!

♪...for ♪
amber waves
of grain...

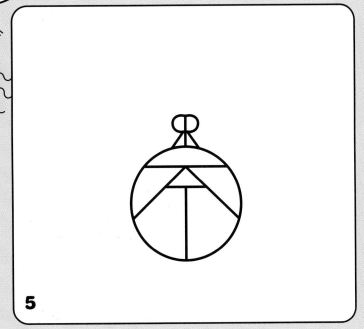

5

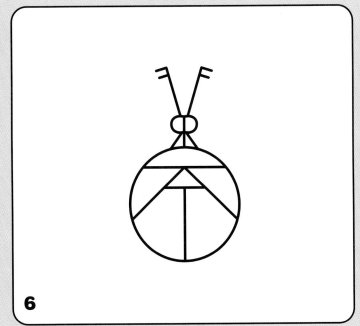

6

O K R **T F** S

Draw a **T** underneath the **K**. Now for antennae, draw an **F** on top of the right **R**. Then draw a backward **F** on top of the backward **R**.

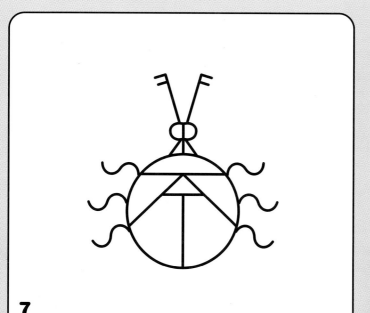

7

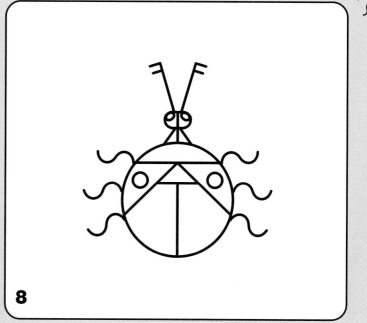

8

O K R T F **S**

Draw three **S**'s on the left side of the body and backward **S**'s on the right side. Now add some **O**'s to the body, and tilted **O**'s for eyes.

Now, if you want, you can squeeze the letters, stretch the letters, fatten the letters using your imagination. Maybe even turn an **O** into a triangle or a square. You can even use lowercase letters — **abcdefghijklmnopqrstuvwxyz.** Design bugs any way you want!